BOOK 2 • ADVANCED

LEARN WITH TUNES

A Melodic Approach to the Violin for Individual or Class Instruction

by CARL GRISSEN

ISBN 978-1-70519-861-2

WILLIS MUSIC

EXCLUSIVELY DISTRIBUTED BY
HAL•LEONARD®

Visit Hal Leonard Online at
www.halleonard.com

World headquarters, contact:
Hal Leonard
7777 West Bluemound Road
Milwaukee, WI 53213
Email: info@halleonard.com

In Europe, contact:
Hal Leonard Europe Limited
1 Red Place
London, W1K 6PL
Email: info@halleonardeurope.com

In Australia, contact:
Hal Leonard Australia Pty. Ltd.
4 Lentara Court
Cheltenham, Victoria, 3192 Australia
Email: info@halleonard.com.au

PREFACE

The Student

In the study of music you will have the helpful advice and the experience of your teacher to guide you safely along the road to good musicianship. But you, as a student, must share with your teacher an equal amount of the responsibility for your own progress. The results achieved will be in proportion to the diligence, the intelligence and the sincerity with which you pursue your studies.

Have definite practice periods, and concentrate your mind upon your work.

Understand, and try to master, the particular points to be accomplished in each lesson.

Review the lesson just passed.

Strive to play easily and with the least amount of effort; avoid lost motion—laborious playing is clumsy playing.

You can best prove your musical intelligence by playing in tune and in time.

Questioning your teacher on various points will help you to understand your work.

Both hands must work in harmony; do not cause one hand to force the other.

Look before you play: *Key, Time, Tempo.*

Count always, and try to look a few notes ahead.

Individual and Class Instruction

We find varying degrees of quality in class as well as in individual instruction. If class groups are too large, or if the members do not receive sufficient individual attention, the best interests of the pupils will not be served. On the other hand, individual instruction without the benefit that is derived from ensemble playing deprives the pupil of valuable training; for the enthusiasm, the spirit of competition, and the youthful zest engendered by this activity are very helpful to both pupil and teacher.

With the object in view of stimulating pupils' interest, a considerable amount of suitably graded ensemble material has been interspersed among the lessons of Book II.

To obviate the unnecessarily prolonged indefiniteness and stumbling of the average pupil in regard to troublesome, unequal fifths, special emphasis has been given to this point. Any further examination of this detail can be made to advantage by turning to the diagram of the G Major scale in two octaves, Lesson 6, where this "break" between the two octaves can be visualized and easily understood.

The following points are recommended for attention during the lesson: key signatures; recitation of scales; la-ing the time when necessary; phrasing; expression; working out principles of the new lesson.

The three T's are still the most important rules: *Tune, Tone* and *Time,* which technically mean the stressing of good intonation, the clear enunciation of tone by good bowing technique, and precision in time and rhythm.

COMMON TERMS USED IN MUSIC

Abbr.	*Name*	*Pronunciation*	*Meaning*
		Relating to Tempo	
Allo.	Allegro	al-lāy′-gro	Lively
	Allegretto	al-la-gret′-to	Lightly—medium fast
	Vivace	ve-vä′-tche	Vivacious—briskly
	Presto	press′-to	Fast
	Animato	an-e-mä′-to	With animation
	Moderato	mo-der-rä′-to	Moderately
	Andante	än-dan′-tay	A moderate, medium tempo
	Andantino	an-dan-tee′-no	Slower, sometimes faster than Andante
	Adagio	ä-dä-sheo	Slowly
	Lento	len′-to	Slow
	Largo	lár′-go	Slowly, broadly
		Changes in Tempo	
accel.	Accelerando	ä-chel-la-ran′-do	Increasing the speed
	Poco a poco	po′-ko a po′-ko	Little by little
	Piu mosso	pee′-oo mos′-so	Quicken the time
	Meno mosso	mā-no mos′-so	Slow the time
string.	Stringendo	string-en′-do	Pressing forward
rit.	Ritardando	ree-tar-dan′-do	Slowing gradually
rall.	Rallentando	räl-en-tän′-do	Gradually slower
allarg.	Allargando	ä-lar-gän′-do	More breadth in time and tone
a.t.	A tempo	ah-tem′-po	Return to regular time
		Relating to Expression	
espress.	Espressivo	es-press-se′-vo	To play with expression
dol.	Dolce	dōl′-tchee	With sweet, subdued tone
	Maestoso	mä-es-tō′-so	Stately, with dignity
	Con spirito	konn spē′-ree-to	Spirited
leg.	Legato	lee-gä′-to	Smoothly, gracefully
ten.	Tenuto	tay-noo′-to	In a sustained manner
dim.	Diminuendo	dē-mee-nu-en′do	Diminishing gradually
		Volume of Tone	
p	Piano	pē-än′-o	Soft
pp	Pianissimo	pe-an-iss′-se-mo	Very soft
mp	Mezzo piano	met′-so pē-än′-o	Medium soft
f	Forte	for′-tay	Loud
ff	Fortissimo	for-tiss′-se-mo	Very loud
mf	Mezzo forte	met′-so for-tay	Medium loud
fp	Forte-piano	fór-tay, pe-än′-o	Loud attack, and immediately soft
sf or ***fz***	Sforzando	sfor-tzän-do	Vigorous accent
cresc.	Crescendo	kra-shen′-do	Gradually increasing tone
decres.	Decrescendo	dā-kra-shen′-do	Gradually decreasing tone
dim.	Diminuendo	de-me-nu-en′do	Gradually diminishing tone
		Various Signs and Terms	
	Segue	say-gwi	Continuing in the same manner
D.C.	Da capo	dä kä-po	Repeat from beginning
D.S.	or Dal segno	dal sen′-yo	Repeat from the sign
	Fine	fee-nay	The end

LESSON 1

Review of the keys of A, D, and G Major

W. B. Whole Bow
H. B. Half Bow
Pt. Point
M. Middle
Fr. Frog
U. H. Upper Half
L. H. Lower Half

A Major

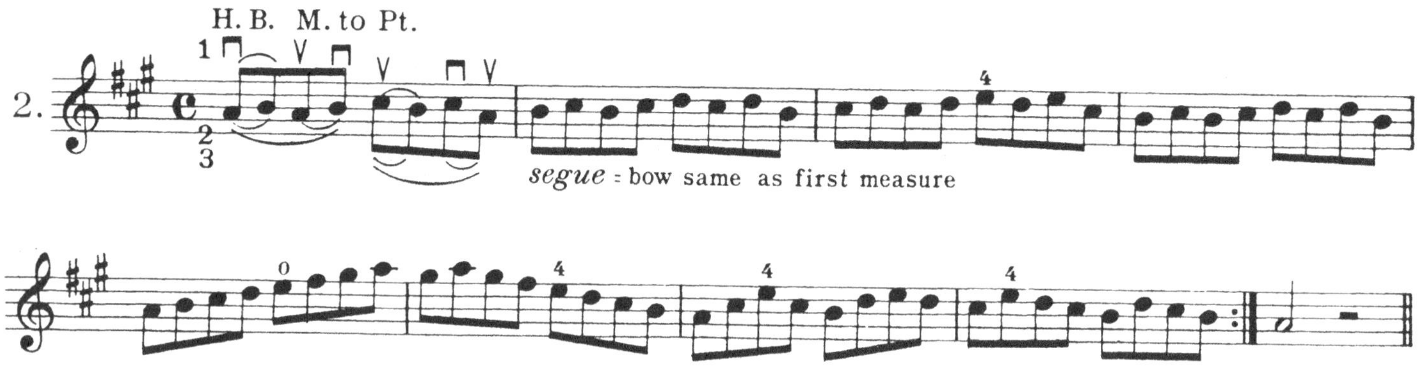

D Major

Use W. B., Pt. and Fr. on this tune

G Major

Play the last three scales and chords from memory.

LESSON 2

Half Tone between the 1st and 2nd fingers

⁀ Sign for Half Tone; fingers close together

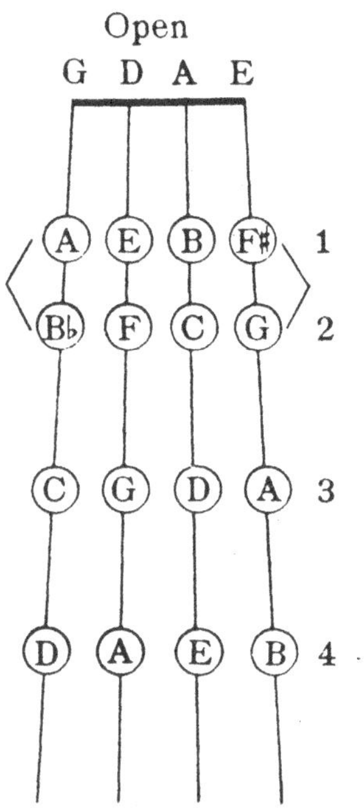

M.

1.

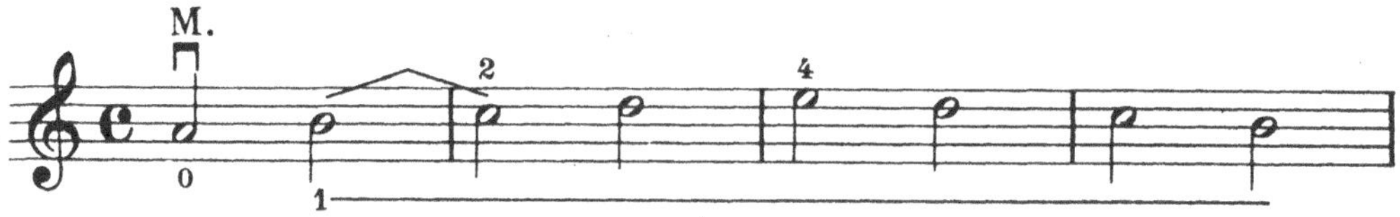

2.

3.

4.

5.

Arabian Song

W. B. C.G.

6.

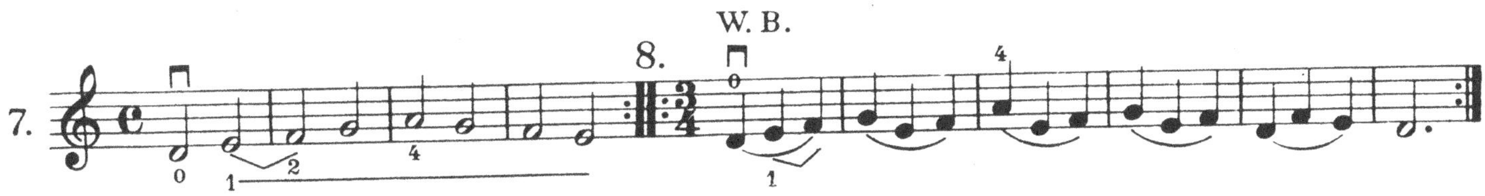

Lightly Row

Eccentric Dance

C. G.

Name the notes on each string which formed the Half Tones in this lesson.

LESSON 3

G Major scale – second octave

1.

2.

Variations on Minuet in G

Moderato

C. Petzold

3.

A Fair Colleen

C. G.

LESSON 4

Key of C Major: also called the Natural Key because it has no sharps or flats. *Always remember* there are only two *natural* half tones: E-F and B-C. All other half tones are made by sharps or flats.

Scale of C Major

1. 

2. 

Old Folks At Home

Moderato (moderately slow)

Foster

3. 

4. 

Boys' Brigade March

C. G.

5. 

LESSON 5

Key of F Major: key signature B♭

A flat (♭) lowers a note a half tone

1.

2.

Auld Lang Syne

Scotch Air

Pupil Andante (rather slowly)

3.

Study in F

C.G.

Allegretto (medium fast)

4.

In Pensive Mood

C. G.

Andante

5.

LESSON 6

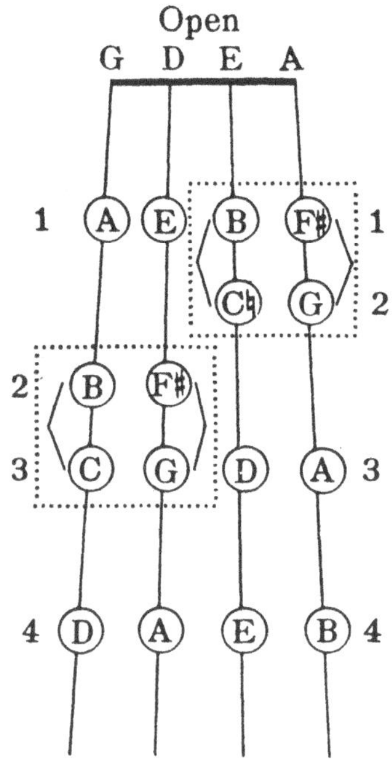

Unequal Fifths

It is very necessary for the student to understand the relationship of perfect and unequal fifths in the study of the violin.

The violin is tuned in perfect fifths: Do-Sol; and any single finger placed on two strings stops a perfect fifth.

Beginning with this lesson we meet with our first unequal fifth. A study of the diagram of the G Major scale in two octaves shows that the relation of tones on the G and D strings is in perfect fifths (straight across from each other) with the half tones between the 2nd and 3rd fingers; and the A and E strings are the same with the half tones between the 1st and 2nd fingers. But the D and A strings are not the same; the 2nd finger must move from f♯ on the D to c♮ on the A string- a half tone downward across strings, or vice versa, a half tone upward. From f♯ to c♮ is an unequal fifth. Unequal fifths occur in every key for one finger or another.

Much time will be saved if the student understands the whole and half tones in each new key, and intonation will be much better if pains are taken to play the unequal fifths carefully.

The G Major scale in two octaves

Combining the half tones between the 1st and 2nd, and 2nd and 3rd fingers.

1.

G Major Chord

The chord of any key is made up of the 1st, 3rd and 5th steps of the scale.

2.

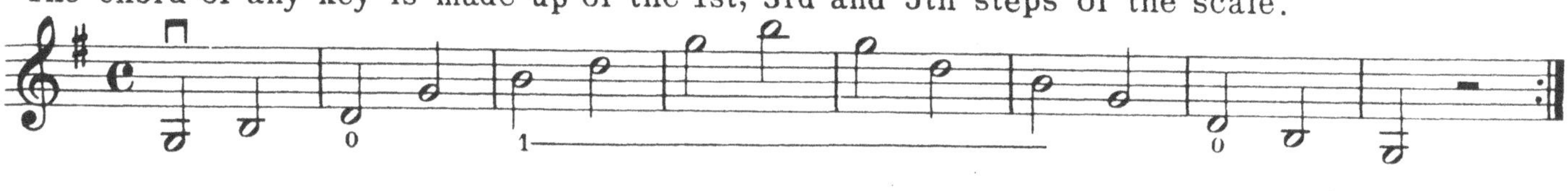

3.

The 2nd finger zigzags from F♯ to C♮.

4.

Be careful of the unequal fifths! F♯ on the D string to C♮ on the A.

5. 6.

Chord Study

7.

Marlive's Waltz

C.G.

Moderato

8.

LESSON 7

America

The Dannebrog

Danish National Air

LESSON 8

Unequal fifths on the G and D strings

The B naturals in No. 2 are used to mark the contrast with the B flats in No. 1; they are not really needed because there are no sharps or flats in the key signature. A sharp or flat appearing in a measure is called an accidental, and holds good for that measure only-unless carried over by a tie.

No. 6 and 7 are the same. The naturals in No. 6 are not needed, but are necessary in No. 7. Why?

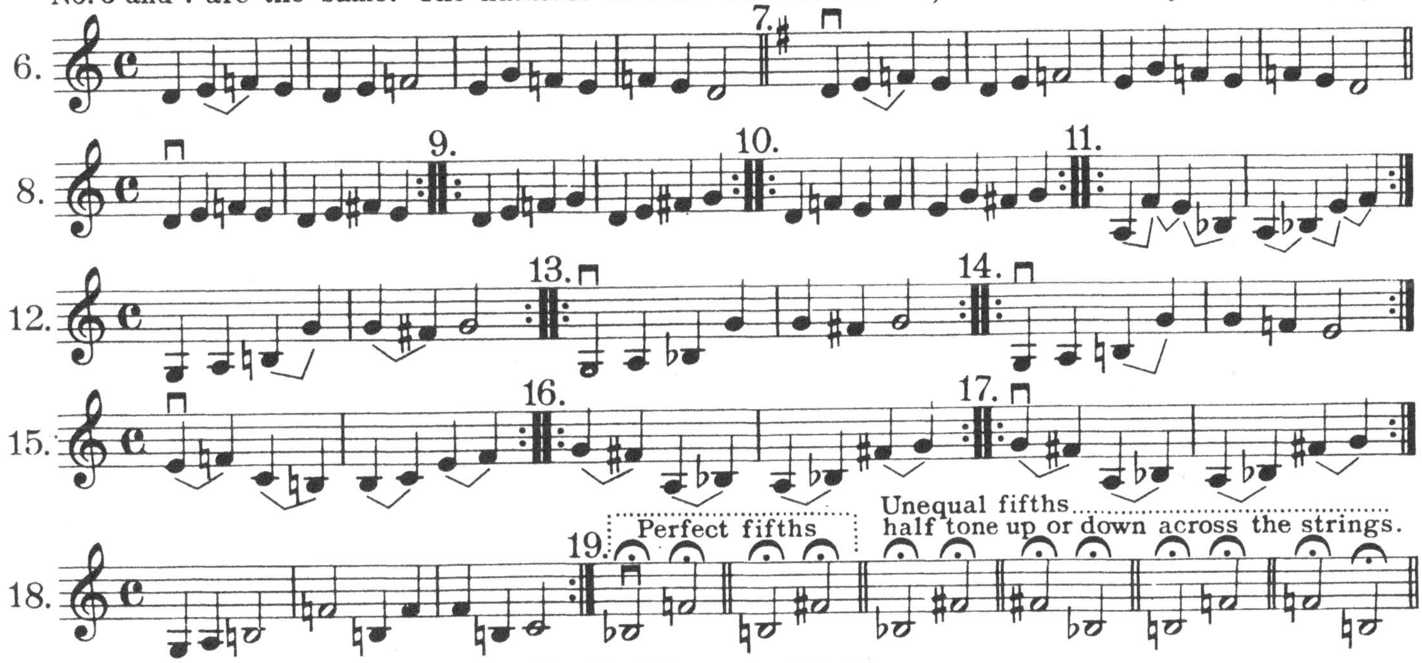

Deft Fingers Waltz

The Twilight Hour

LESSON 9

Unequal fifths or chromatic (half tone) shifting of the 2nd finger on the A and D strings

Gently Gliding

German Folk Song

LESSON 10

Unequal fifths on the A and E strings

Etude (study)

C.G.

German Folk Song

LESSON 11

German Folk Song

Spring Morning

C.G.

*This sign (>) means to accent the note.

LESSON 12

Half tone between the open E string and the 1st finger
E to F. Key of C Major

Keep the hand straight-bend the 1st finger back at the third joint without tilting the hand forward. When the 1st finger plays a half tone from the nut stretch the 4th finger well to reach its note.

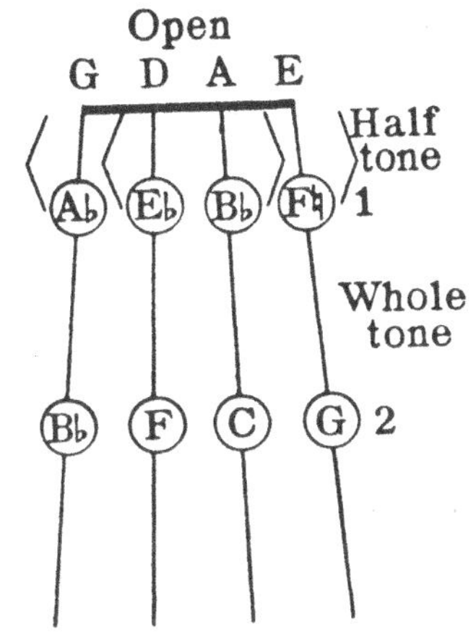

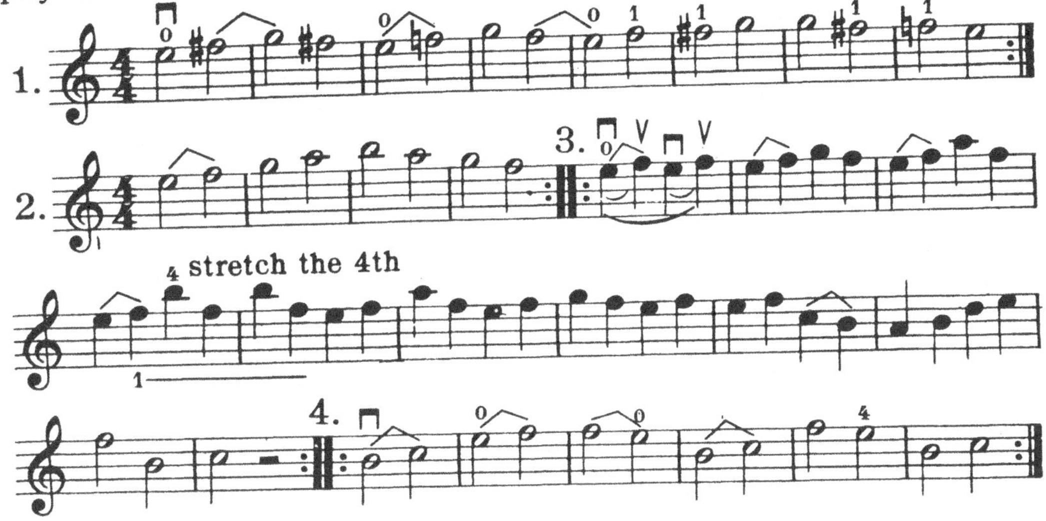

The Wheel Goes Round

Echo

C.G.

Festival March

C.G.

LESSON 13

Half tone between the open A string and the 1st finger
A to B♭. Key of F Major: key signature one flat: B♭

The Lorelei

German Folk Song
Silcher

*This sign is called the Fermata or Hold; hold the note longer than the time value calls for. Used for the sake of expression.

LESSON 14

Half tone between the open D string and the 1st finger
D to E♭. Key of B♭ Major: key signature two flats: B♭ and E♭

In Nos. 3 and 4 B♭ and E♭ are written in. In Nos. 5 and 6 B♭ and E♭ are flatted by the key signature.

In The Gloaming

Harrison

Lively Spirits

C. G.

* Rallentando–holding back the time.
** Place the 1st finger on both notes at the same time.

LESSON 15

Review of the keys of C, F and B♭ Major

*The Lass Of Richmond Hill

Allegretto — English Folk Song

Now try playing this song in a light, flowing style with the bow-arm perfectly relaxed.

Chord Study

Class Honors

Marziale (with martial spirit) — C. G.

Happy Moments

Allegretto — C. G.

*An important problem in this piece is the unequal fifth, B♮ on the A string to F♮ on the E. Make the 1st finger do the work of bending back to F♮ in order that the correct position of the hand will not be disturbed.

LESSON 16

$\frac{6}{8}$ Time

6 = Six counts to the measure
8 = An eighth note gets one count
In slow and moderate time count six, and in faster time count two to the measure.

An eighth note (♪) = one count
A quarter note (♩) = two counts (beats)
A dotted quarter (♩.) = three beats
A dotted half (𝅗𝅥.) = six beats

Play these on the open string while counting aloud.

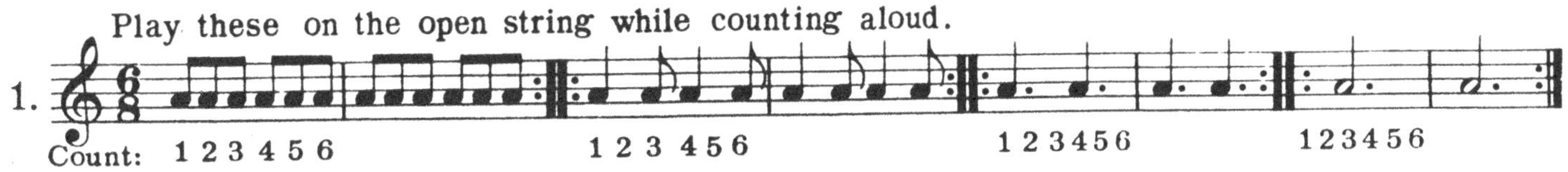

Apply the following examples in slow and quick time to exercise No. 2

Oats and Beans

The Mulberry Bush

For He's A Jolly Good Fellow

Old French Tune

*D. C. Da Capo (go to the beginning), and end at **Fine (the end).

LESSON 17

Three Blind Mice

Whistling Tom

C. G.

LESSON 18

Important Rules:
1. Study the key signatures that you may know which notes are flatted or sharped.
2. Note the Time signature and strive to keep good time.
3. Music is lifeless without good rhythm which comes from good time and accentuation.

Pop Goes The Weasel

Sweet and Low

Barnby

Goodbye, My Lover, Goodbye

*fz forzando (sharp accent)
**rallentando e diminuendo (retard and diminish)

LESSON 19

Review of the open and 1st, 1st and 2nd, 2nd and 3rd finger half tones on the A and E strings. Do not change position of the hand: slide 1st and 2nd fingers without raising from the string.

The Minor Mode

Songs in the Major, joy of life;
Songs in the Minor, sorrow and strife.

Stretch the 4th finger

Stretch the 4th finger

16.

Every Major key has a relative Minor key; (same key signature). The 6th and 7th steps of the minor scale are raised in the ascending and lowered in the descending scale.

The scale of A Minor: relative minor of C major.

17.

Autumn Shadows

C. G.

Andante

19.

Cossack Dance

C. G.

Vigoroso (vigorously)

20.

LESSON 20

Open and 1st, 1st and 2nd, 2nd and 3rd finger half tones on the D and G strings.

The scale of D Minor: relative minor of F Major.

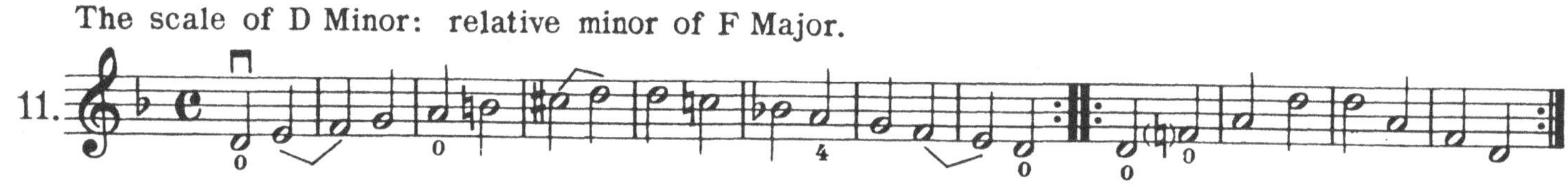

Russian Lullaby

Andantino (moderate tempo) C.G.

13.

15.
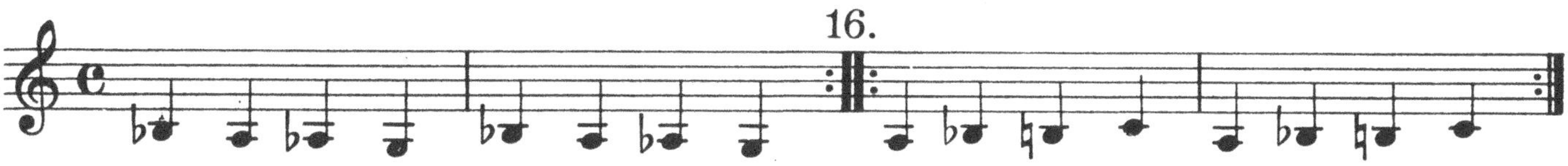

17.

The scale of G Minor: relative minor of B♭ Major.

19.
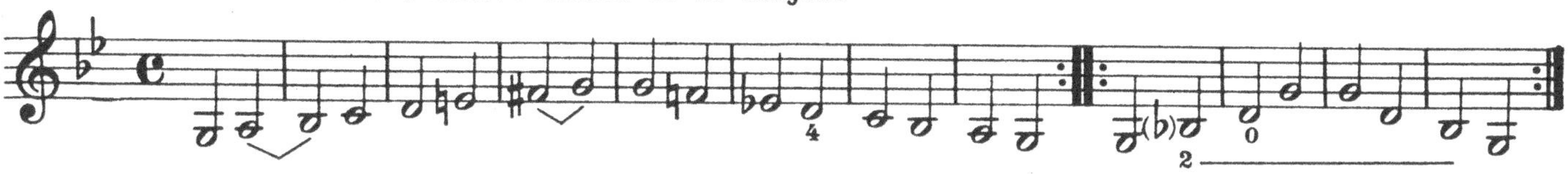

Beautiful Minka

Russian Folk Song

LESSON 21

The Spirit of Christmas

Christmas Tidings

C.G.

Deck The Hall

Old Welsh Carol

It Came Upon The Midnight Clear

Willis

LESSON 22

Syncopation

Syncopation—the tying of one beat, or partial beat over to another beat.

Whole beat syncopated; beats 2 & 3 tied together.

Fractional part of beat syncopated.

Keep the fingers down.

Shufflin' Along

C. G.

Tenting On The Old Camp Ground

Kittredge

LESSON 23

The Triplet

The Triplet is a group of three notes equal to one beat in any quarter time: $\frac{2}{4}$: $\frac{3}{4}$: $\frac{4}{4}$.

As a rule the numeral *3* is placed above the group, but not always. Remember, the triplet must be played to a single beat; not counted separately like the similar grouping in $\frac{6}{8}$ time.

1. 

2. 

March of the Dwarfs

C.G.

3. 

4. 

Diagram showing the 1st finger tones a half tone from the nut and the flatted 4th finger notes.

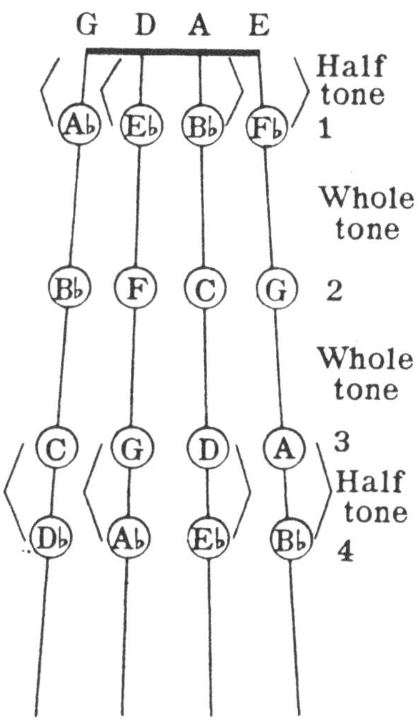

No open E string: see diagram.

5.

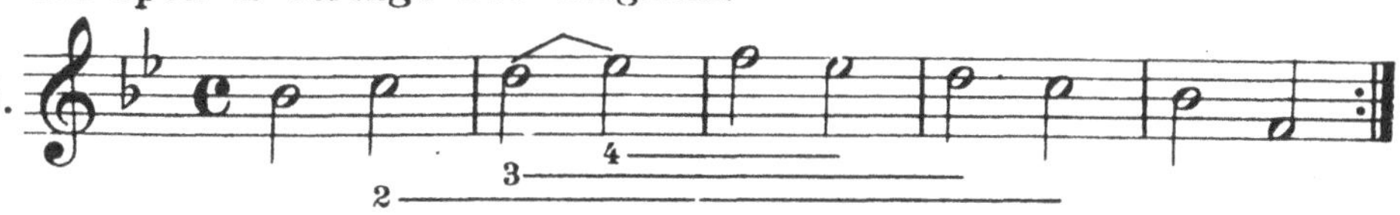

Scale of B♭ Major: Hand straight–reach back with the 1st finger.

6.

7.

O Come, All Ye Faithful

J. Reading

8.

It is suggested that easy assignments of double-stopping begin at this point. Nos. 1 and 2 of Lesson 34 may be assigned with this lesson.

LESSON 24

When beginning with any of these 2nd finger tones the student will gain in accuracy by placing the 1st finger, then measuring the 2nd from this tone.

The B♭ Major scale in two octaves–low to high B♭.

1. 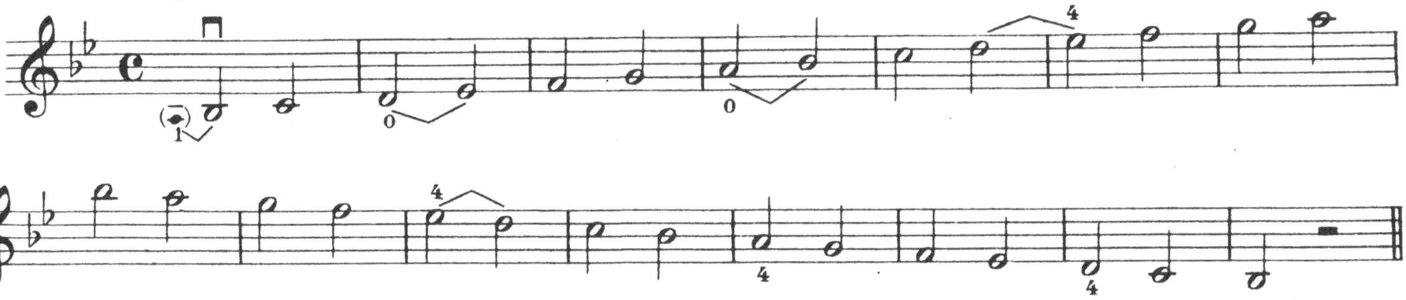

2. 

3. 

4. 

Song of Good Cheer

Allegretto

C.G.

5. 

Review March

C.G.

6.

What points are reviewed in this piece? Musical figure? Time? Key?

German Folk Song

7.

Nos. 3 and 4 of Lesson 34 may be studied with this lesson.

LESSON 25

Key of E♭ Major: key signature three flats: B♭, E♭, A♭. No open A or E strings.

Scale of E♭ Major

Old Dog Tray

(Refrain)

Foster

5.

Key of A♭ Major: key signature four flats: B♭, E♭, A♭, D♭. No open D, A or E strings.

Scale of A♭ Major

6.
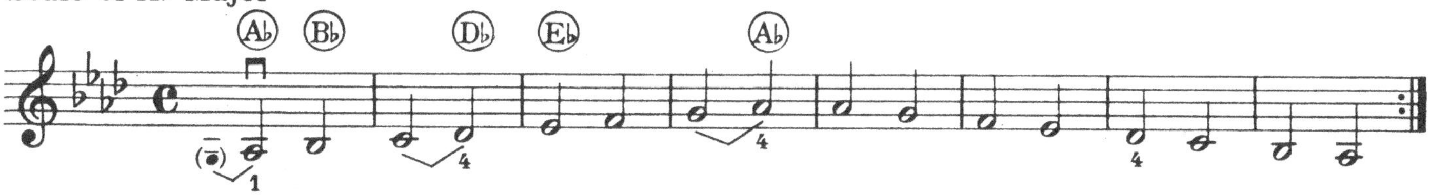

7.
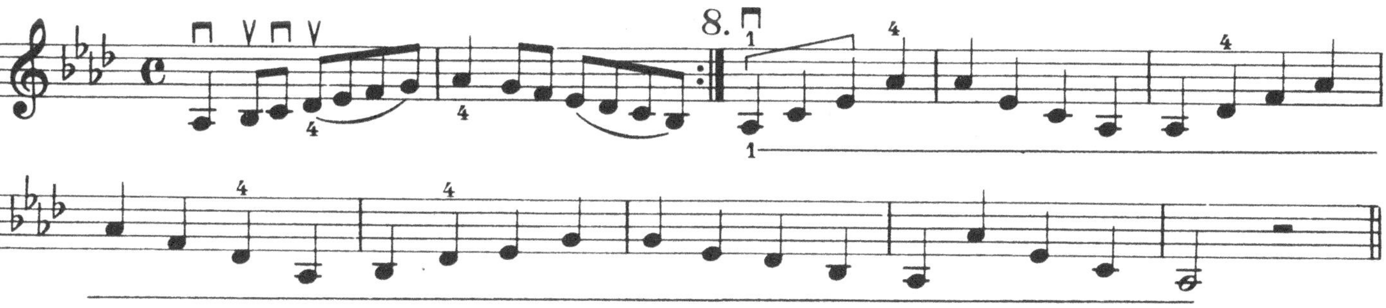

9.

Roll, Jordan, Roll

Andante

Spiritual

LESSON 26

Sixteenth Notes

A single sixteenth note is written with two hooks (𝅘𝅥𝅯): two or more notes are connected by two beams (♬).

Sixteenth notes are sometimes abbreviated as follows:

1. 

Eighth and sixteenth notes are often combined in the following manner:

This common figure (♩. ♬) may be represented by pronouncing the word 'light-ly'.

Sixteenth rest.

2. 

Practice the following examples on the open string then apply them to the bowing exercise below; No. 4. Use little bow in the middle. Play the sixteenth notes evenly without hurrying.

3. 

Use the above bowings on exercise No. 4: (a) and (i) will show how to do it.

U. H. Play the sixteenth note with a light wrist stroke as a slight extension of the longer first note.

Bowing Exercise

4. 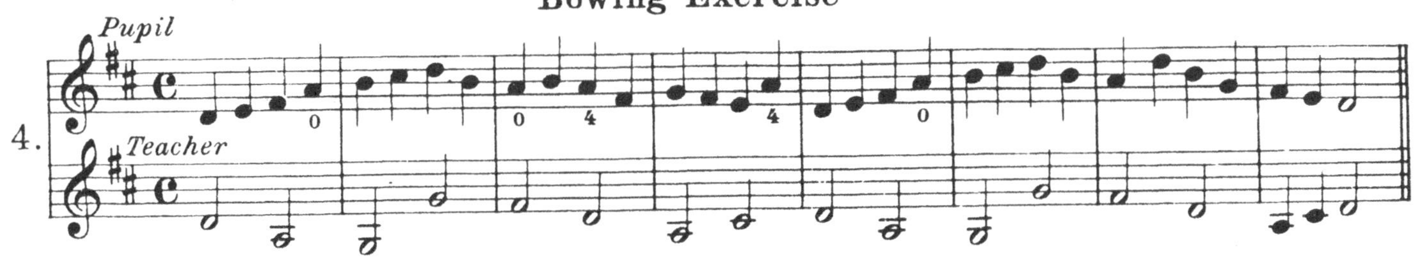

Try, Try Again

C. G.

5. 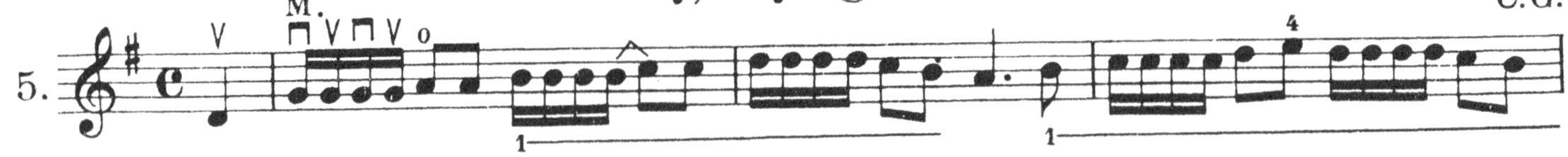

LESSON 27

Ring de Banjo

Allegretto

Foster

The Last Rose Of Summer

Andante cantabile (in a singing style)

Old English Air

Turkey In The Straw

Allegretto

American Tune

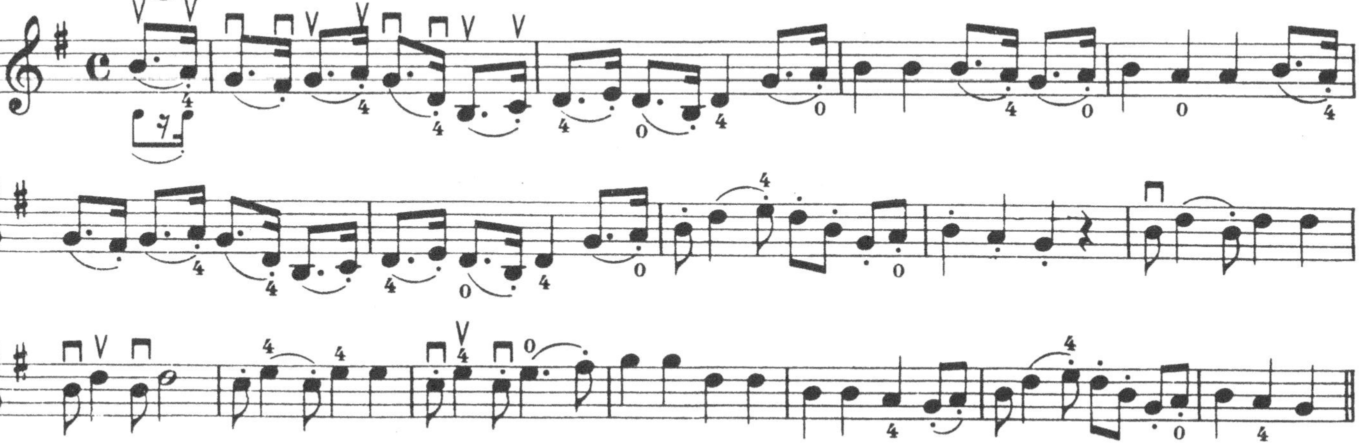

Assign Nos. 5 and 6, Lesson 34 with this lesson.

LESSON 28

Key of E Major: key signature four sharps: F♯, C♯, G♯, D♯

Which strings can not be played open in this key? Stretch the 3rd finger well for the sharped 3rd finger notes.

Diagram of the E Major scale

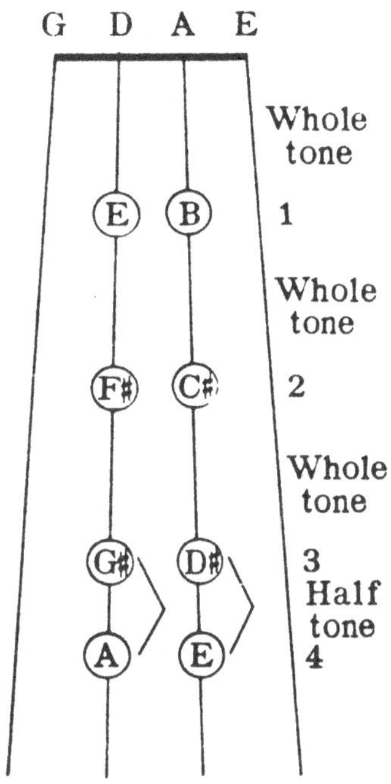

Scale of E Major

1.

4.

The First Nowel

Traditional

*The Minstrel Boy

Old Irish Air

*Play this beautiful melody with plenty of bow, and a full, singing tone.

LESSON 29

Key of A Major: key signature three sharps: F♯, C♯, G♯

Elbow well under the violin, and stretch the 3rd finger for C♯ and G♯.

Scale of A Major

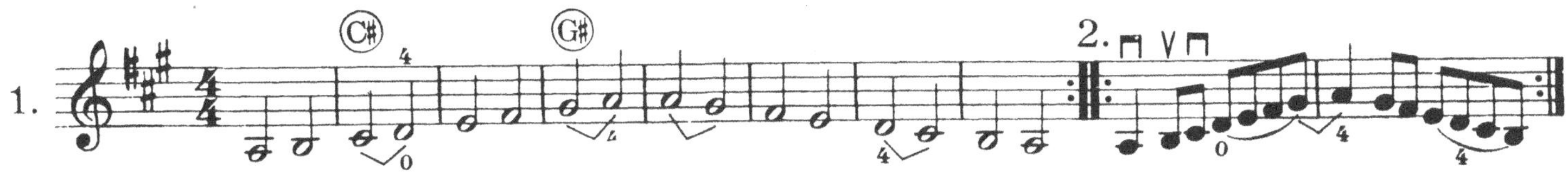

Clown Dance

Moderato

C. G.

Scale of A Major in two octaves

Look out for this unequal fifth!

7. 

Tyrolienne

C.G.

Assign Nos. 7 and 8, Lesson 34 with this lesson.

LESSON 30

In lesson 25 the lower octave of the A♭ Major scale was studied; now look at the key diagram and you will notice that the 2nd and 3rd fingers play the half tones in the upper octave.
The student should *recite* each scale before playing it.

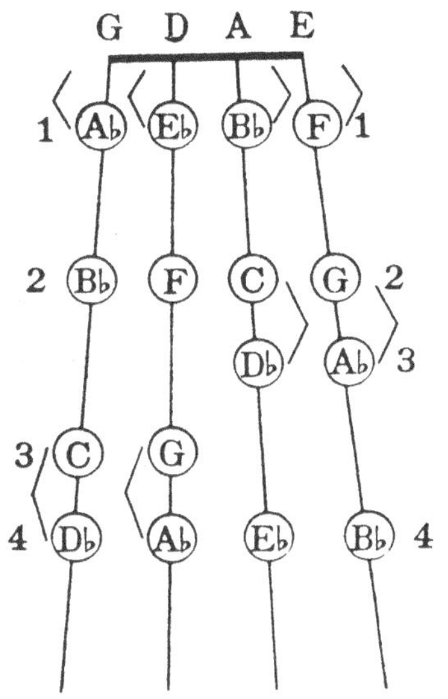

The scale of A♭ Major: the G is the only open string in this key.

1. 

2. 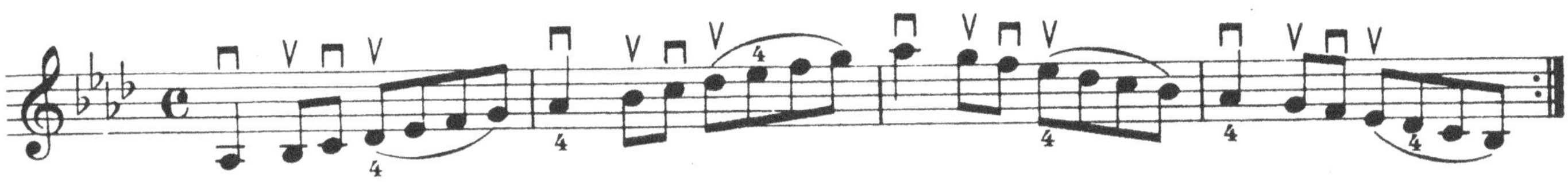

3. 

4. 

Every key has its unequal fifths: observe them carefully for good intonation.

6. 

Through The Woods

C. G.

Believe Me, If All Those Endearing Young Charms

Irish Air

LESSON 31

The note grouping  played in Lesson 30 in slow tempo must now be studied in fast time. To understand the rhythmical swing of this figure pronounce the word Am-ster-dam to one beat of the foot.

Preliminary Exercise

Practice with slow, medium, and fast time to learn the bowing.

Three Jolly Hunters

C.G.

Assign Nos. 9 and 10, Lesson 34 with this lesson.

LESSON 32

Enharmonic tones and the Chromatic scale

Enharmonic tones (the same tone written differently).
The Chromatic scale is a scale of half tones.

When Chromatic scale stays on one string use the 3rd finger twice.

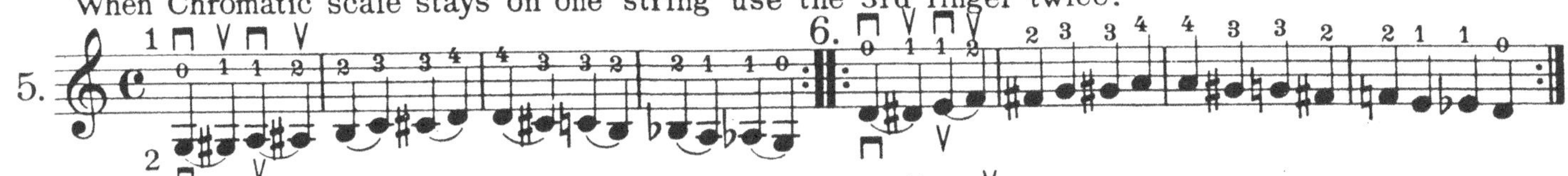

Move 3rd finger well up for sharped note.

When Chromatic scale moves beyond one string use the 4th finger for the sharped 3rd finger note.

LESSON 33

Pizzicato – Cut Time

Pizzicato (abbreviated pizz.) means to pluck the string with the 1st finger of the right hand. Hold the bow with the 2nd, 3rd and 4th fingers leaving the thumb and forefinger free: place the thumb about an inch from the upper end of the fingerboard and pluck the notes with the forefinger. ARCO (bow) Use the bow again.

Variation on Twinkle, Twinkle, Little Star

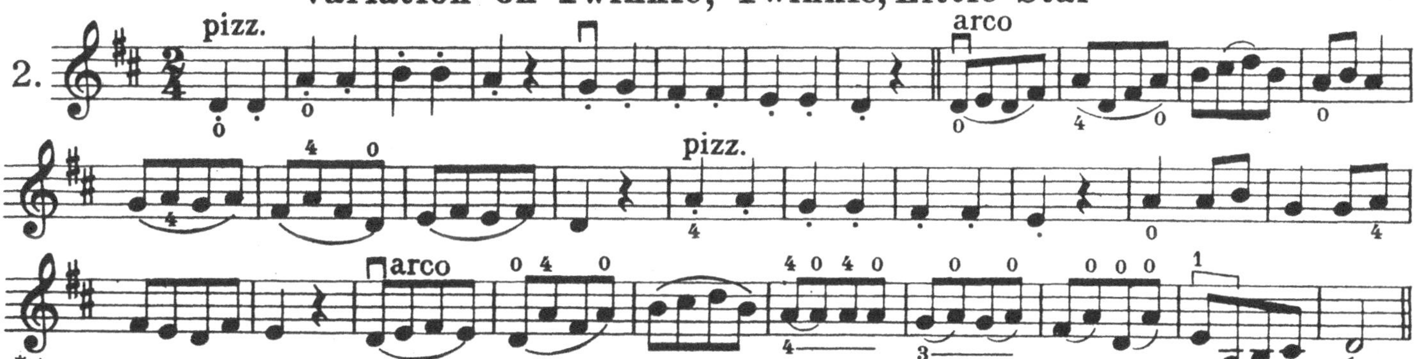

*𝄵 signifies Alla Breve or Cut Time. $\frac{4}{4}$ is cut in half. Two quarters or a half note get one beat, and there are two counts to the measure.

Cross Country March

Pupil Allegro

C. G.

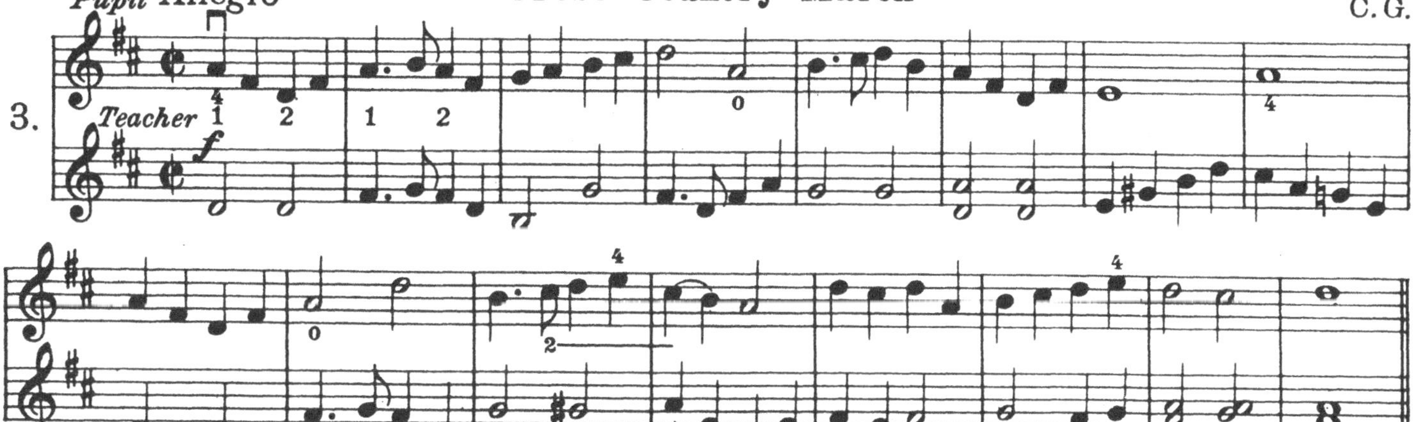

The Twilight Hour

Pupil Andante

C.G.

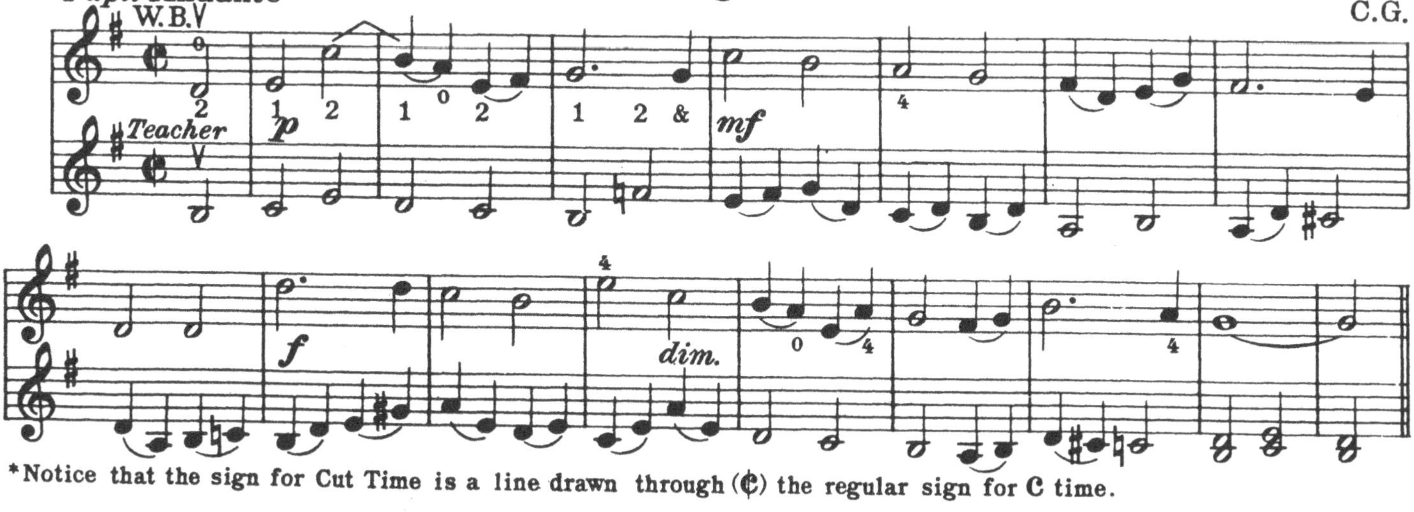

*Notice that the sign for Cut Time is a line drawn through (𝄵) the regular sign for C time.

LESSON 34

Double Stopping

(playing two notes at the same time)

Draw the bow evenly on the two strings, use little pressure, and keep the arm relaxed. Move the fingers carefully across the strings to their respective tones.

Thirds

Sixths

Chorale

C. G.

LESSON 35

Double Stopping, continued

Chords

Two Against One

Harmony Waltz

C. G.

Chords

Draw the bow straight

Review Piece

C.G.

LESSON 36

*Mazurka Maxine

C. G.

*Mazurka – a Polish dance characterized by strong rhythm and accents.